COLD
PASTA

COLD PASTA

JAMES McNAIR

Photography by Tom Tracy

Chronicle Books • San Francisco

Art direction, photographic and food styling, and book design by James McNair

Editorial assistance by Lin Cotton

Book design consultation by Alan May

Photography assistance by Chris Saul

Typography and mechanical production by Terrific Graphics

Cover: Angel Hair with Three Caviars, see pages 30-31.

Printed in Japan.

Library of Congress Cataloging in Publication Data

McNair, James.
    Cold Pasta.

Includes index.
    1. Cookery (Macaroni)
    2. Cookery (Cold Dishes)
    I. Title
TX809.M17M39 1985 641.8'22
    85-363
ISBN 0-87701-353-5

Distributed in Canada by
Raincoast Books
112 East Third Avenue
Vancouver, B.C. V5T 1C8

12 11 10 9 8

Chronicle Books
275 Fifth Street
San Francisco, California
94103

For Lin Cotton, my partner and soul mate in this life, with eternal gratitude for his absolute love and unqualified friendship, for sticking by me through both the rough times and the joyous occasions, and for encouraging me to find and believe in myself.

ACKNOWLEDGEMENTS   To everyone at Chronicle Books for their fine work on both the original and revised versions of this book. Special thanks to Larry Smith, publisher at the time of the first edition, who first believed in our combined potential.

To Sharon Silva for her expert copyediting.

To Alan May for helping me turn my design notions for this book series into actuality.

To Sue Fisher King for the loan of so many beautiful dishes and linens from her imaginative San Francisco shop.

To Richard Burton for the original cover photograph used in the sales catalog.

To Tom Tracy for capturing my food creations on film, to his wife and manager Barbara for keeping everything organized, and to his assistant Chris Saul for invaluable contributions.

To John Carr for the use of his marvelous kitchen and unique dishes, and especially for introducing Joshua J. Chew and Michael T. Wigglebutt into our lives during the original photography of this book.

To friends who loaned props and physical assistance as I styled the photographs for this book while recuperating on crutches following knee surgery, especially to Larry Heller, Louis Hicks, Ken and Christine High, the Tad Highs, Stephen Marcus, Alan May, Marian May, the Bob Spences, and William Tikunoff.

To Mike Tucker for his computer expertise.

To my secretary Addie Prey and my testing assistant Buster Booroo for their valuable assistance.

Contents

Introduction

Long before the current American infatuation with cold pasta, the Japanese slurped icy noodles with crispy vegetables while the Chinese enjoyed cold sesame-dressed noodles. Generations of southern Italians passed on a few traditional recipes for hot-summer cold pasta as we continued to make family favorite macaroni salad variations.

However, it has taken good old American ingenuity to develop these simple ideas into a new food that is not only fashionable, but also delicious enough to turn those modest dishes into classics that are likely to stay.

Today cold pasta is hot! Americans are now eating cold or, more accurately, room-temperature pasta by the tons. Pasta salads have swiftly become standard fare for picnics, buffets, parties, and lunches. Cold new ways with pasta run the gamut from brown-bag treats to first courses at the most elegant dinner party. These innovations are even making their way to Italy, where restaurants are hesitantly adding cold pasta to their summer menus, albeit mainly for American tourists.

The cold pasta phenomenon coincides with the blossoming American creativity with great food and especially with the proliferation of takeout fancy food shops. Room-temperature pastas that are easily prepared, hold up well, and transport successfully have quickly become staples of that business genre.

While many takeout shops, restaurants, and caterers offer superb versions of cold pasta, many imitators unfortunately have not had as much respect for quality. Too many mushy, tasteless, or unattractive concoctions have given cold pastas a bad reputation in some circles.

When cold pastas are made with the highest quality and freshest ingredients, they're just as satisfying and as much fun to eat as their hot counterparts.

The first time I ever saw or tasted a cold pasta was back in the 1970s when I began a continuing obsession with Italian foods. Instead of throwing away the excess unsauced *spaghettini* dinner one night, I stuck it in the refrigerator. At lunchtime the next day I threw in some fresh vegetables, olives, capers, cheese, and a little oil and vinegar. Suprisingly, it was love at first bite. Over the next year or so this recipe evolved into a warm-weather staple around my house.

My partner Lin Cotton and I later opened Picnic Productions International, Inc., a company specializing in fanciful to outrageous picnics. One of the first enterprises of the fledgling PPII was to prepare seven hundred spectacularly packaged individual picnics to sell at a San Francisco parade. My old standby pasta salad scooped into see-through containers became a major component. If you haven't made enough tubs of pasta to feed seven hundred, you're missing one of life's rare experiences. Measuring herbs by the cups and oil and vinegar by the gallon is guaranteed to make preparing a dinner party for ten to twenty seem like child's play.

On a gloriously sunny Sunday morning, behind the wheel of a pickup truck piled high with a mountain of pink-and-white-packaged picnics, Lin and I went off to conquer the palates of San Francisco. Since our potential patrons had yet to read of how chic it could be to eat cold pasta, in disappointment we gave away most of the beautiful lunches with the strange new food. Those brave souls who did taste were filled with compliments and questions and a few became loyal patrons.

In preparation for opening a retail picnic store, Lin and I headed for

Fancy food takeout shops have helped make cold pasta hot in America.

New York and Europe on a scouting expedition. While checking out the new stores that had opened since I moved west from the Big Apple, I was thrilled to discover The Silver Palate, an exciting new addition to my old neighborhood. Among the offerings of fresh foods from owners Julee Russo and Sheila Lukins were a variety of cold pastas.

A visit to Los Angeles with my friend Jon Gould introduced me to his mother's successful Pasta Pasta Pasta. Her array of takeout pasta salads remain among the best I've tasted. Today she and Jon together operate Pasta Etc., continuing to create Italian versions of cold pastas.

My old standby pasta salad recipe appeared in my book *Adventures in Italian Cooking.* Then needing to expand my cold pasta repertoire during the two years Lin and I operated Twin Peaks Grocery and its catering sideline, I developed a number of new ideas for cold pastas.

Many of my professional party planning experiences with cold pasta proved fun, although nothing topped a party for Steve Silver's musical revue, *Beach Blanket Babylon.* To match the style of the show's outlandishly oversized hats, we bought four-foot wide, bowl-shaped baskets, sprayed them bright colors, lined them with heavy-duty plastic, and heaped them up with Italian-style cold pastas. The filled baskets, presented on a flower-bedecked buffet, were in a scale that would rival a Rose Bowl parade float.

As I write this book and retest my collection of cold pasta recipes from Twin Peaks Grocery and my catering ventures and create new dishes, it's snowing furiously outside the windows of my office and kitchen at Lake Tahoe. I'm reminded of my catering era discovery that cold pasta doesn't have to be reserved for warm weather.

Little hand-held bowls of Pasta with Fresh Corn and Lima Beans in

Apple Cider Vinaigrette as prelude to a recent December supper brought back memories, fragrances, and tastes of happy summer days. Likewise, I've found Saffron-laced Pastina with Currants, Pine Nuts, and Mint a tasty accompaniment to autumn's roasted or smoked fowl. Pasta Shells Stuffed with Scallop Seviche make a good beginning to a meal no matter what the season. The curry spices and coconut in Vermicelli with Shrimp in Curried Yogurt Dressing are as appropriate on a Christmas buffet as they are on the beach.

After all, crisp cold salads of greens, vegetables, or potatoes are enjoyed all year long. Why not the same year-round enjoyment from appetizers, soups, salads, main dishes, and even desserts made of cold pastas.

A search through recent cookbooks and food magazines turned up only a handful of cold pasta recipes. As far as can be determined, this is the first book devoted to pasta dishes designed to be eaten at room temperature or slightly chilled. Use it with enjoyment as a basis for your own creative cooking.

Technique

With only a few minor alterations, the techniques for cooking hot pasta are all you need to know to follow the recipes in this book successfully and to create your own cold pastas.

CHOOSING PASTA

For many hot dishes, nothing can be more satisfying than impeccably made fresh pasta. When cooled and tossed with dressings, however, freshly made pasta tends to absorb too much liquid, becoming soft and mushy.

If you are in the habit of making your own pasta from hard durum wheat flour or semolina, you may still choose to make the pasta ahead and dry it for use in dishes that are to be served cold. I feel this is a total waste of time, however, since better results can be achieved with the many excellent factory-made dried pastas that are readily available.

When choosing shapes and sizes for cold pastas, keep in mind that *fettuccine, rigatoni, lasagne,* and other thick or bulky noodles are best eaten hot. Cold, they seem like chewy blobs. Likewise, stuffed pastas, although available as cold dishes in some takeout fancy food shops, are unsatisfactory since the fillings tend to be gummy when served cold or at room temperature.

The array of available shapes of good dried pasta can keep any creative cook from using the same shape twice for a long time. Most of us, however, find a few favorites that we enjoy repeating often.

ITALIAN PASTA

There's little agreement among Italians when it comes to what to call the various forms of dried pasta. The same name can apply to a variety of shapes and sizes, or the same shape can have several names depending on the region where it is made or used. To further confuse the matter, the name changes when you add ridged surfaces *(rigati)*, curly edges, or flavors and colorings such as tomato, spinach, or beet. If a

The author often prepares cold pastas the night before to allow flavors to fully develop.

15

name ends in *-oni* the pieces are large, while *-ini* at the end means they are small.

No matter the shape or size, dried pasta dough is basically all the same: flour and water, sometimes enriched by eggs. Of course, the type and quality of the flour can vary greatly, resulting in different cooking times and degrees of firmness. Pasta made from hard durum wheat flour retains more texture when cooked than that made from other wheats. For the dishes in this book, look for products made of durum wheat flour, preferably from Italian factories.

AMERICAN PASTA   Most American-made dried pastas are packaged under the Italian names for shapes and sizes. Although a few excellent ones are now being manufactured, the majority of dried pastas made in the United States are so easily overcooked that I cannot wholeheartedly recommend their use. You can, however, achieve satisfactory results if you carefully watch the cooking time and then chill immediately to halt the cooking process.

American egg noodles enriched with egg yolks are manufactured in a variety of widths and shapes that range from tiny forms resembling bits of barley or Italian soup *pastina*, to the traditional broad egg noodle that is usually cut into short pieces. Properly cooked, these egg noodles can be satisfactorily used for many of the recipes in this book. I prefer them to other pastas for dishes that are baked, such as Noodle Pie with Spicy Cajun Ham or Noodle Pudding with Vanilla Bean Sauce. Look for high-quality, good-textured brands especially made for Jewish cookery.

Dried pastas are manufactured in scores of shapes and sizes.

ORIENTAL PASTA

Not quite as confusing namewise as their Italian counterparts, a number of Oriental noodles work well in cold dishes.

Mein. Chinese noodles are long strands of flour and water paste enriched with egg and available dried, fresh, or frozen. Unlike fresh Italian pastas, these noodles tend to stay firm enough after their brief cooking to make fresh ones acceptable for cold dishes.

Japanese Noodles. A variety of dried Japanese noodles are excellent for cold dishes. *Soba* are long, thin tan noodles made from buckwheat; green tea is sometimes added to the buckwheat flour for color and flavor. *Somen* is a thin hard wheat flour noodle, often made with egg yolk. *Udon* are rounded thicker noodles; choose the thinnest version you can find. Precooked instant Japanese noodles, often labeled *ramen*, are best reserved for hot dishes.

Cellophane Noodles. These thin, chewy noodles made of mung-bean starch have a transparent or jellylike appearance when cooked. On their own, they are almost without flavor, though they quickly absorb flavors of dressings or cold sauces. Look for them under other picturesque names: shining noodles, spring rain, bean threads, silver threads, long rice, pea starch, or *fun see.*

Soak the wiry bundles of cellophane noodles in warm water for twenty-five to thirty minutes, then cut with kitchen scissors to desired lengths before boiling. They can also be fried without soaking and used as a crunchy topping or snack.

Rice Sticks. These transparent dried noodles made from rice look like cellophane noodles. When quick fried, they make crispy toppings or snacks. Presoaked and boiled, they can be used as any other pasta. Wiry rice sticks are sometimes labeled *mai fun* or rice *vermicelli.*

Noodles from the Orient offer variety to cold pasta dishes. Use them interchangeably with more familiar Italian counterparts.

COOKING PASTA

Always cook pasta in ample boiling water: four quarts per pound is the standard ratio. Pasta cookers with removable colanders are designed to hold sufficient water and to make cooking and draining easy. Any large pot will work as well. Have a colander large enough to comfortably hold the pasta standing by in the sink.

Some cooks advocate adding normal or extra amounts of ordinary table salt or coarse salt to the cooking water for pasta that is to be served cold. The salt certainly doesn't affect proper cooking and with the current emphasis on reduced sodium intake, I feel it is a matter best left to the cook's discretion. If you do choose to salt the water, wait until it comes to a boil. Presalted water takes longer to boil, and thus uses more energy. Remember, too, most of the salt gets thrown out with the water or rinsed off when you quick-cool the pasta.

Always bring water to a brisk boil before dropping in pasta all at once. Briskly stir with a long-handled wooden spoon to activate water and separate strands or pieces. With long noodles or large chunky shapes, you'll need to stir several times during the cooking. If the strands are too long to be completely immersed, just drop them upright into the

Drop pasta all at once into briskly boiling water (left) and stir well to prevent it from sticking. Pull strands from water (right) to taste-test for doneness.

water, wait a few seconds until the ends soften, and then gently push the remaining pasta under the water.

Biting into the pasta is the only way to tell when it is done. Pasta for cold dishes should be cooked slightly less than you're accustomed to cooking pasta that is to be served hot. I've identified the desired texture as very *al dente*. Practice will teach you when it has the proper tenderness, yet remains firm enough to hold up to vinaigrettes, oil dressings, or mayonnaise additions, all which tend to make pasta soft.

The very second the pasta tests done to your preference, drain it well, then cool to room temperature before combining with other ingredients. Although I'd never think of rinsing pasta for hot dishes, I find most pastas for cold dishes, especially thin noodles and tiny shapes, turn out best when quick-cooled by rinsing in plenty of cold water. Drain well once again before pouring into a large bowl for mixing.

Drain cooked pasta in a colander (left). For most recipes in this book, quickly cool cooked pasta under cold water (right) to halt cooking and keep it from sticking together until ready to mix with other ingredients.

Instead of rinsing, well-drained warm large shapes or *spaghetti*-sized pasta can be tossed with a little oil or dressing in a large bowl. While the pasta cools to room temperature, stir occasionally to coat it

thoroughly and to keep it from sticking together. This method allows the pasta to absorb more of the flavors of the dressing base. I often toss Oriental noodles with soy sauce prior to the oil to give them a rich color as well as flavor.

Once cool, you can elect to complete the dish or to refrigerate the pasta and mix it with other ingredients a bit later. If doing the latter, let the pasta return to room temperature before proceeding.

INGREDIENTS

Cold pastas should emphasize freshness. Raw or partially cooked fresh vegetables add crispness as well as flavor and color. Tiny peas or lima beans are the only vegetables I find acceptable—and almost as good—frozen; just thaw and add them uncooked. All vegetables should be cut into bite-sized or smaller pieces.

By all means, make your own dressings. In this book I've given pasta-to-dressing proportions for each recipe. Pastas, however, vary in their ability to retain firmness. Some may require more or less dressing, or your own preference may be for more or less. If you find that the amount of dressing in a recipe does not suit your taste, make a note and next time adjust the measure accordingly. The length of time the pasta stands prior to serving also affects the amount of dressing needed. Should you find the pasta underdressed at the point of serving, add a bit more of the basic dressing ingredient: oil, mayonnaise, yogurt, or sour cream.

If you like pastas only lightly dressed, consider passing extra dressing or sauce at the table for those who prefer more.

Strong flavors such as anchovies, capers, fresh coriander (cilantro), and garlic should be used with discretion. If I don't know the tastes of my guests, I use these strongly flavored ingredients in small amounts, then pass little dishes of them at the table for those who love these flavors.

The same goes for hot pepper of all types. Perhaps my palate is jaded from growing up on zippy Louisiana foods and my dad's heavenly (he's a Baptist minister, after all), yet devilishly spicy, barbecue, but I'm a confirmed pepperholic. Szechuan chili oil, Louisiana red hot sauce, chilies fresh or canned, cayenne, peppercorns in black, white, green, or pink—I love them all in great quantity.

If you feel differently or don't know your guest's tastes, I advise using peppers judiciously. Therefore, I have not recommended specific amounts in any recipes. One thing to bear in mind, however, is that cold pasta absorbs a lot of heat, as well as a lot of flavor, so you may need to "overseason" foods. But it is much better to play it safe to begin with; you can always pass more of the spicy ingredients at the table.

I've also given no specific measurements for salt in these recipes. It should be added according to taste. Catering and running a gourmet store taught me to cut way back or even eliminate salt, letting people add to suit their palate or dietary requirements.

Always taste cold pastas after they've sat for a bit and had time to absorb flavors. Correct the seasonings before serving. In some cases, I've indicated passing additional seasonings such as sesame oil, chili oil, or soy sauce.

STORING Many cold pastas taste best after resting a few hours. Those with oil-based dressings that do not contain perishable meats can remain in a cool place while flavors develop. Others should be refrigerated. Most will keep up to three or four days, many of them improving as flavors blend and mellow.

When you make cold pastas ahead and refrigerate them, always cover well. Return them to room temperature or almost that point before serving. Pastas with crunchy vegetables should be stored without these additions. Toss them in just before serving.

Do not refrigerate pastas with sour cream dressings such as Angel's Hair with Three Caviars; the pasta turns to a sticky mass. Toss and serve at the last minute.

When transporting cold pastas to picnics or other events, exercise the same care as you would with any food. If they contain fish or other highly perishable ingredients, take them on ice. Vinaigrette-dressed vegetable pastas can remain unrefrigerated for several hours, although during hot spells the food may taste better if it has been kept refrigerated until about thirty minutes before serving.

SERVING TEMPERATURE　　Perhaps this book should have been titled *Room-Temperature Pasta*. As I've repeated throughout, the majority of these dishes taste best at room temperature or only slightly chilled, not icy cold. Be sure to take them out of refrigerated storage in time to reach the proper temperature for prime taste. Specific directions are included with those few dishes that are best when served chilled or on ice, such as Iced Clear Noodles with Toppings and Dipping Sauce.

PORTIONING　　Whenever I develop recipes, I have great difficulty putting down an exact number of people the dish will serve. Some people eat like my sister Martha and a normal recipe would serve twenty; others, like my friend Tad, can practically demolish the entire recipe.

With hot pasta, I always use as rule of thumb one-fourth pound per person if it is the main course, and one-eighth pound per person if it is a first course. Cold pastas run much the same, although pasta salads that contain a lot of vegetables can be stretched further, with a pound of pasta serving twelve or more. Trial and error will help you determine how much your crowd can eat.

Most of the recipes in this book are based on one pound of pasta and as salads or accompaniments serve from eight to ten to twelve. I chose to go with these party-sized recipes since pasta salads are generally prepared for entertaining and ingredients are fairly inexpensive. Left-overs can be stored for later in the week.

PRESENTATION Cold pastas may be arranged on individual plates in the kitchen and presented elegantly at the table. Or you may opt to put the food on a serving platter or large bowl from which you serve at the table or allow everyone to help themselves.

No matter what style of presentation you use, it is important to note that some dishes taste delicious but can look like dog food once you stir in a dressing. Since appearance is just as important as taste, I often save out a few of the main ingredients to arrange on the top.

When you serve pasta on individual plates, remember smaller is better. Leave everyone wanting more. You can always scoop up seconds from the kitchen.

With garnishing, understatements are usually more effective than lily gilding. Small pieces of fresh vegetables, edible flowers, nuts, canned pimiento, pickles of all sorts, olives, or tiny greens from the garden (everything from baby spinach to carrot tops) make presentations more appetizing, but shouldn't overwhelm.

Pasta Shells
Stuffed with Scallop Seviche

12	ounces firm white scallops, cut into very small pieces
1	cup (or more) freshly squeezed lime juice
½	cup finely chopped red onion
1	small ripe tomato, peeled and chopped
2–3	fresh hot chili peppers, finely chopped
¼	cup vegetable oil
2	tablespoons white wine vinegar
1	teaspoon granulated sugar
½	cup fresh coriander (cilantro) leaves, coarsely chopped
	Salt
	Freshly ground black pepper
12	ounces large (not jumbo) pasta shells
	Fresh coriander (cilantro) sprigs (garnish)

As an easy alternative to stuffing, toss one pound cooked tiny shell pasta with seviche and the accumulated juices and serve as a salad or first course.

1. To make *seviche*, place scallop pieces in a ceramic or glass container and add just enough lime juice to cover. Refrigerate at least 5 hours (but no more than 24 hours), stirring several times.

2. Add onion, tomato, chilies, vegetable oil, vinegar, sugar, chopped coriander, and salt and pepper to taste to scallops. Toss gently, cover, and refrigerate until assembly time, as long as overnight.

3. Drop shells into 4 quarts boiling water, stirring gently to prevent sticking. Reduce heat to medium and cook, uncovered, stirring frequently but very gently, until shells are very *al dente*, about 10 to 12 minutes after water returns to a boil. Drain shells and place in a large bowl of cold water to cool for about 5 minutes. Discard any that tore during cooking. Place the good shells (slight tears are okay) in a bowl, cover with damp paper toweling, and refrigerate about 30 minutes.

4. Drain seviche, spoon into pasta shells, and arrange stuffed shells on a tray. Garnish with coriander sprigs and let stand a few minutes before serving.

Serves 10 to 15 as appetizer; 8 as first course.

NOTE: Always cook more shells than you think you'll need, since some will tear or lose their shape. Carefully follow the cooking and cooling instructions, which differ slightly from those for other dried pastas. The trick seems to be not to cook shells as long as other pastas. Cooling in water, resting in the refrigerator, and the absorption of the filling juices further soften the shells.

Spicy Fried Rice Sticks

1   pound rice *vermicelli*,
       broken into 3-inch lengths
       Peanut or vegetable oil
       for frying
       Salt
       Flavored salts:
       garlic, onion, celery
       Herbal salt substitutes
       Cayenne pepper
       Freshly ground
       black pepper
       Paprika
       Curry powder

Deep fry Asian rice vermicelli, known as rice sticks or mai fun, then sprinkle with seasonings while still hot. Store noodles in tightly covered containers for up to several weeks. They're ready for snacking at cocktail or any other hour.

1. Pour 2 to 3 inches of oil in a wok or frying pan. Heat oil to 350° F and drop in small handfuls of noodles; turn noodles quickly with two spoons while they instantly puff up and become crisp. Remove from pan with a slotted spoon as soon as they stop crackling; drain on paper toweling.

2. While still hot, sprinkle noodles with any of the suggested or other favorite seasonings to taste, alone or in combination. When cool, store in a tightly covered container until ready to serve.

Makes 6 to 8 cups.

Angel's Hair
with Three Caviars

8   ounces *capelli d'angelo* (angel's hair) or other very thin pasta

2   tablespoons vegetable oil

1/3   cup minced fresh chives

2   hard-cooked egg yolks, finely chopped

1/4   cup sour cream

2   tablespoons freshly squeezed lemon juice

3/4   cup whipping cream

3   ounces (or more) *each* golden, red, and black caviar

Choose the best caviar your budget allows for this very elegant beginning to a warm-summer dinner. Keep portions small.

1. Cook pasta in 4 quarts boiling water until very *al dente*. Drain and rinse well in cold water, then drain again. Place in a large bowl and toss with vegetable oil, stirring occasionally to keep pasta from sticking together.

2. Gently combine most of the chives and chopped egg yolk (reserve some of each for garnish) with the pasta.

3. Just before serving, blend together sour cream, lemon juice, and whipping cream, then mix thoroughly but gently with the pasta. Do not refrigerate; the sauce and pasta will become a gooey mass if you do.

4. Arrange the pasta on individual plates and spoon on dollops of caviar, putting a portion of each color on each serving. Garnish with reserved chives and egg yolks.

Serves 4 to 6 as first course.

Noodle Pie
with Spicy Cajun Ham

8	ounces thin egg noodles, broken into small pieces
3	tablespoons butter
2	cloves garlic, minced or pressed
4	eggs
1	cup finely diced *tasso* (spicy Cajun smoked ham), or other cooked ham
½	cup grated white Cheddar cheese
2	tablespoons minced fresh parsley
½	teaspoon *each* dried thyme and oregano leaves
2	teaspoons paprika
	Salt
	Liquid hot pepper sauce
	Cayenne pepper
	Freshly ground black pepper
	Sliced canned pimiento (garnish)
	Fresh parsley leaflets, preferably Italian (garnish)

Present small wedges of this chilled pie as an appetizer. For finger food that will be passed, I like to bake the pie in a square pan and then cut it into small squares for serving.

1. Cook noodles in 2 quarts boiling water until very *al dente*. Drain and rinse well in cold water, then drain again.

2. Melt butter in a small pan, add garlic, and sauté over moderately low heat until limp, but not browned. Reserve.

3. Beat eggs well in a large bowl. Add reserved garlic and butter, tasso or ham, cheese, minced parsley, thyme, oregano, paprika, and salt, liquid hot pepper, cayenne, and black pepper to taste. This dish should be spicy, so be generous with the peppers. Add noodles, mix well, and pour into a buttered 10-inch quiche or pie pan.

4. Bake at 350° F until firm and lightly browned on top, about 35 minutes. Cool, then cover with foil or plastic wrap and refrigerate until well chilled. To serve, cut into thin wedges; garnish each wedge with a bit of pimiento and a parsley leaflet.

Serves 8 to 10 as appetizer.

Pasta with Lobster in Tangy Tarragon Mayonnaise

3/4 pound *cavatelli* (short, crinkle-edged shells) or other fancifully shaped pasta

3 tablespoons chopped fresh tarragon

2 tablespoons chopped fresh parsley

Cayenne pepper

1½ cups homemade mayonnaise

2 live lobsters (about 2 pounds each), cooked, shelled, and meat cut into bite-sized pieces (reserve shells for garnishing)

Salt

Freshly ground black pepper

Thinly sliced radishes (garnish)

Fresh tarragon sprigs (garnish)

Pasta and lobster meat garnished with brightly colored shells make a showy dinner opening or main course for an outdoor lunch.

1. Cook pasta in 3 quarts boiling water until very *al dente*. Drain and rinse well in cold water, then drain again. Place in a large bowl and cool to room temperature, stirring occasionally to keep pasta from sticking together.

2. Add chopped tarragon, parsley, and cayenne pepper to taste to the mayonnaise and mix well with pasta. Add lobster meat and season with salt and black pepper to taste. Serve slightly chilled or refrigerate as long as overnight. Remove from refrigerator about 30 minutes before serving; add a little more mayonnaise if mixture is too dry.

3. Serve pasta garnished with reserved lobster shells, radishes, and tarragon sprigs.

Serves 8 as first course or salad; 4 as main course.

Pasta with Smoked Salmon in Dill Dressing

⅓ cup safflower oil

1½ tablespoons minced shallots

2 tablespoons freshly squeezed lemon juice

⅓ cup chopped fresh dill
Salt
Freshly ground black pepper

8 ounces *gemelli* (twisted twin rods) or other fancifully shaped pasta

1 cup ripe cherry tomatoes, halved

¼ cup minced fresh chives

5 ounces (or more) smoked salmon, cut into small pieces

1 small red onion, thinly sliced in rings, and rings separated

1 cup sour cream
Fresh dill sprigs (garnish)

Lazy summer weekend brunches or lunches are appropriate times for this one.

1. Combine oil, shallots, lemon juice, chopped dill, and salt and pepper to taste; whisk well and set aside.

2. Cook pasta in 4 quarts boiling water until very *al dente*. Drain and rinse well in cold water, then drain again. Place in a large bowl and cool to room temperature, stirring occasionally to keep pasta from sticking together.

3. Add tomatoes, chives, and reserved dressing to the pasta and mix gently. Arrange salmon, onion rings, and sour cream on top of pasta. Garnish with dill sprigs.

Serves 4 to 6 as first course or salad.

Avgolemono Soup
with Pastina

6   cups homemade chicken
      stock, or 4 cups canned
      chicken broth diluted with
      2 cups water
1   cup *pastina* (tiny pasta)
3   eggs
¼   cup freshly squeezed
      lemon juice
      Salt
      Freshly ground
      white pepper
      Lemon slices (garnish)
      Finely minced fresh parsley
      (garnish)

This favorite Greek soup is usually made with rice and served hot. Tiny soup pastina adds a new dimension and chilling offers a refreshing lemony opening to summer dining.

1. Heat chicken stock or broth to boiling. Stir in *pastina* and cook until very *al dente*, about 5 minutes. Remove from heat.

2. Beat eggs in a small bowl until pale yellow and frothy, then beat in lemon juice. Slowly drizzle about 2 cups of the warm stock into the egg-lemon mixture, whisking constantly until mixed well.

3. Add the egg-lemon mixture to the remaining warm broth, whisking constantly to avoid curdling of the egg. Add salt and pepper to taste. Cool to room temperature, then refrigerate until serving time, up to 24 hours.

4. Just before serving, stir soup and pour into bowls. Garnish with lemon slices and a sprinkling of parsley.

Serves 10 to 12 as first course; 4 to 6 as main course.

Iced Clear Noodles with Toppings and Dipping Sauce

¼ cup rice wine vinegar

2 tablespoons plus 1½ teaspoons sugar

Salt

1 cup reconstituted *dashi* or regular-strength canned chicken broth

¼ cup *mirin* (Japanese sweetened rice wine) or sherry

⅓ cup soy sauce

1 medium-sized cucumber, peeled and sliced paper thin

8 ounces cellophane noodles (bean threads)

1 cup cooked crab meat

6 ounces firm *tofu* (soybean cake), cut into bite-sized pieces

1 cup finely shredded *daikon* (white radish)

20 fresh whole chives

2 tablespoons *wasabi* (Japanese horseradish powder), mixed with water to make a paste

½ cup sliced pickled ginger

4 ounces fresh *enoki* mushrooms (optional)

2 ounces canned ginko nuts (optional)

One of the most cooling dishes you can serve on a hot day, this soup-salad relies on Japanese clear noodles made from mung beans. Use chopsticks to pick up noodles and toppings for dipping into individual bowls of sauce. In place of the cellophane noodles, choose somen (very thin Japanese wheat noodles) or any thin pasta. Dashi, fish and kelp stock, is availble in instant forms in Japanese markets.

1. Combine vinegar, 2 tablespoons sugar, and ¼ teaspoon salt in a small saucepan and heat, stirring, just to dissolve sugar. Set aside.

2. To prepare dipping sauce, mix *dashi* or chicken broth, *mirin* or sherry, soy sauce, and the remaining 1½ teaspoons sugar in a small saucepan and simmer, stirring, until sugar dissolves. Chill.

3. Sprinkle cucumber slices with salt and rub the salt into the slices with your hands. Set aside for 30 minutes, then squeeze out liquid.

4. Pour reserved vinegar dressing over cucumbers and mix thoroughly. Set aside for about 15 minutes.

5. Soak noodles in warm water for about 25 minutes, cut into 3-inch lengths with kitchen scissors, then cook in 3 to 4 quarts boiling water until very *al dente*. Drain and rinse in several changes of cold water, leaving noodles in the last bowl of rinse water until ready to serve.

6. At serving time, place noodles in individual shallow bowls filled halfway with cold water and several cubes of ice. Drain cucumber slices and arrange them on a tray with crab, *tofu, daikon,* chives, *wasabi,* pickled ginger, enoki mushrooms, and ginko nuts. Let everyone select favorite toppings to add to bowls of noodles. Distribute dipping sauce among small individual bowls or cups at each place. Use chopsticks (or forks) to dip salad into sauce.

Serves 6 to 8 as soup-salad; 4 as main course.

Pasta with Fresh Basil, Tomato, and Parmesan

12 ounces *radiatore* (crinkled curls) or other fancifully shaped pasta

½ cup olive oil

2 tablespoons freshly squeezed lemon juice

1½ cups firmly packed chopped fresh basil

3 cups chopped very ripe Italian plum tomatoes

¾ cup freshly grated Parmesan cheese

Salt

Freshly ground black pepper

Fresh basil leaves (garnish)

Nothing could be simpler or more delicious than this crisp taste of the Italian summer garden.

1. Cook pasta in 4 quarts boiling water until very *al dente*. Drain and toss with olive oil and lemon juice. Cool to room temperature, occasionally stirring the pasta to coat thoroughly.

2. Add chopped basil, tomatoes, cheese, and salt and pepper to taste to the pasta. Mix thoroughly but gently. Garnish with basil leaves.

Serves 8 to 10 as salad.

Macaroni with Tomato, Cucumber, Feta Cheese, and Greek Olives

¾ cup olive oil
2 tablespoons freshly
   squeezed lemon juice
2 cloves garlic, minced
   Salt
   Freshly ground
   black pepper
1 pound macaroni
3 medium-sized ripe
   tomatoes, peeled and
   coarsely chopped
1 small cucumber, peeled,
   halved, seeded, and sliced
1 small red onion, chopped
¼ cup chopped fresh parsley,
   preferably Italian
6 ounces feta or other
   goat cheese, crumbled
   Anchovy fillets (garnish)
   Kalamata or other
   Greek olives (garnish)

A combination that evokes daydreams of warm Greek isle summers.

1. Combine ½ cup olive oil, lemon juice, garlic, and salt and pepper to taste. Reserve.

2. Cook macaroni in 4 quarts boiling water until very *al dente*. Drain and toss in a large bowl with the remaining ¼ cup olive oil. Cool to room temperature, occasionally stirring the pasta to coat thoroughly.

3. Add tomatoes, cucumber, onion, and parsley to macaroni and mix well. Add reserved dressing and mix thoroughly. Gently stir in most of the cheese, reserving some for garnish. Garnish with anchovy fillets, olives, and remaining feta cheese.

Serves 10 to 12 as salad.

Saffron-laced Pastina
with Currants, Pine Nuts, and Mint

¼ teaspoon ground saffron
(optional)

½ cup olive oil

2 cloves garlic,
finely minced or pressed

3 tablespoons freshly
squeezed lemon juice

¼ teaspoon ground cumin

2 teaspoons ground turmeric

1 teaspoon granulated sugar
Salt
Freshly ground
black pepper

1 pound *semi di melone*
(melon-seed shape) or
other *pastina* (tiny pasta)

⅔ cup pine nuts,
lightly toasted (see note)

½ cup currants, plumped in
hot water for about 20
minutes and drained

¼ cup *each* chopped fresh
mint and parsley

3 tablespoons chopped fresh
coriander (cilantro)
Fresh mint sprigs or
leaves (garnish)
Pomegranate seeds
(optional; garnish)
Orange blossom water
(optional)

Tiny pastina, most often used in soups, approximates the ubiquitous couscous of North African cuisine. The slight sweetness makes this a good side dish with roasted or grilled meats.

1. Dissolve saffron in olive oil and let stand about 15 minutes. Add garlic, lemon juice, cumin, turmeric, sugar, and salt and pepper to taste. Set aside.

2. Cook pasta in 3 quarts boiling water until very *al dente*. Drain and rinse well in cold water, then drain again. Place in a large bowl and toss with saffron-flavored oil. Cool to room temperature, occasionally stirring the pasta to coat thoroughly.

3. Add pine nuts, drained currants, chopped mint, parsley, and coriander to pasta. Serve at room temperature garnished with mint sprigs or leaves and pomegranate seeds, if available. Sprinkle lightly with orange blossom water just before serving.

Serves 10 to 12 as salad or side dish.

NOTE: To toast pine nuts, place them in a small heavy frying pan over moderate heat. Stir until they begin to turn golden. Remove from heat and pour onto a plate to cool.

Penne with Provençal Eggplant and Sweet Peppers

2	medium-sized eggplants, unpeeled and cut into 1-inch cubes
1	cup olive oil Salt
2	medium-sized onions, sliced
3	red, green, or gold sweet peppers, thinly sliced
4	cloves garlic, finely minced or pressed Freshly ground black pepper
¼	cup freshly squeezed lemon juice
2	teaspoons dried *herbes de provence*
1	pound *penne* (quill-shaped tubes)
1½	cups firmly packed chopped fresh basil Fresh basil leaves (garnish)

You can almost smell the basil, lavender, and rosemary that permeate the air of southern France when you eat this dish.

1. Place eggplant cubes in a shallow baking pan, toss with ½ cup olive oil, sprinkle with salt to taste, and bake in a 400° F oven until cubes are soft but still hold their shape, about 30 minutes. Set aside to cool.

2. Heat ¼ cup olive oil in a large heavy frying pan. Add onions and sweet peppers and cook over very low heat until vegetables are quite tender and slightly caramelized, about 35 to 45 minutes. Stir in garlic and salt and pepper to taste; cook 5 minutes longer.

3. Combine the remaining ¼ cup olive oil, lemon juice, *herbes de provence*, and salt and pepper to taste. Whisk and reserve.

4. Cook pasta in 4 quarts boiling water until very *al dente*. Drain and rinse well in cold water, then drain again. With a sharp knife, diagonally slice each piece of pasta in half crosswise. Toss in a large bowl with onion mixture and reserved dressing.

5. Toss eggplant cubes and chopped basil with pasta. Garnish with basil leaves.

Serves 6 to 8 as first course; 10 to 12 as salad.

Pasta Rings
in Spicy Cucumber Raita

2	medium-sized cucumbers, peeled, seeded, and coarsely grated
2	tablespoons minced or grated yellow or white onion
	Salt
2	cups plain yogurt
1	clove garlic, minced or pressed
2	green onions, chopped
1	small tomato, finely chopped
2	tablespoons freshly squeezed lemon or lime juice
2	tablespoons finely minced fresh mint or parsley
2	teaspoons ground cumin
	Freshly ground black pepper
1	pound *anellini* or other small pasta rings
	Fresh mint or parsley sprigs (garnish)
	Cucumber slices (garnish)

Raita is a cold yogurt-based condiment in Indian cuisine. Tossed with pasta, it is a cooling side dish with spicy meats.

1. Combine grated cucumber and onion in a small bowl. Sprinkle with salt and let stand for 10 minutes. Drain and squeeze dry.

2. Whisk yogurt until creamy smooth. Add cucumber mixture, garlic, green onions, tomato, lemon or lime juice, minced mint or parsley, cumin, and salt and pepper to taste and mix thoroughly. Chill as long as overnight.

3. Cook pasta in 4 quarts boiling water until very *al dente*. Drain and rinse well in cold water, then drain again. Place in a large bowl and cool to room temperature, stirring occasionally to prevent pasta from sticking together.

4. Combine pasta with yogurt mixture. Garnish with mint or parsley sprigs and cucumber slices.

Serves 10 to 12 as side dish.

Pasta with Fresh Basil Pesto

2 cups firmly packed fresh basil leaves, washed and dried

3 cloves garlic

½ cup pine nuts

¾ cup freshly grated Parmesan cheese

¼ cup freshly grated Romano cheese

½ cup plus 3 tablespoons olive oil

1 pound *ruote* (cartwheels) or other fancifully shaped pasta

Fresh basil leaves (garnish)

Pasta al pesto is an all-time favorite hot dish. It's also delicious as a cold summertime salad. If you don't have fresh basil, please choose another salad.

1. Combine 2 cups basil leaves, garlic, and ⅓ cup pine nuts in a blender or food processor and purée to desired smoothness. Add ½ cup Parmesan and the Romano cheese and blend briefly. Pour in ½ cup olive oil and mix well. Set aside.

2. Cook pasta in 4 quarts boiling water until very *al dente*. Drain and toss in a large bowl with the remaining 3 tablespoons olive oil. Cool to room temperature, occasionally stirring the pasta to coat thoroughly.

3. Mix reserved pesto with pasta. Garnish with the remaining pine nuts and fresh basil leaves. Serve at room temperature.

Serves 10 to 12 as salad.

Buckwheat Noodles
with Asparagus in Sesame Dressing

1   cup soy sauce
¼   cup reconstituted *dashi*
       (see package directions) or
       homemade chicken stock
       or regular-strength canned
       chicken broth
1   tablespoon granulated
       sugar
3   tablespoons sesame seeds,
       toasted (see note)
1   pound dried *soba*
       (buckwheat noodles) or
       other thin noodles
1   pound fresh young
       asparagus, cut diagonally
       into 1-inch pieces
       (reserve a few whole spears
       for garnishing)
6   green onions,
       cut diagonally into
       ½-inch pieces
       Fresh *shiso* (minty
       Japanese herb) leaves
       (optional; garnish)

Japanese buckwheat noodles team up with fresh young asparagus in a simple traditional salad dressing made with dashi, a fish and kelp stock available in instant forms in Japanese markets. Chicken broth makes an acceptable substitute. Linguine can be used in place of soba and green beans can alternate with asparagus.

1. In a blender or food processor, combine soy sauce, *dashi* (made according to package directions), sugar, and 1½ tablespoons sesame seeds and blend until smooth. Set dressing aside.

2. Cook noodles in 4 quarts boiling water until very *al dente*. Drain and toss in a large bowl with reserved dressing. Cool to room temperature, occasionally stirring the noodles to coat thoroughly.

3. Cook asparagus in boiling water until crisp-tender. Plunge immediately into ice water to stop cooking. Drain well, then add to pasta along with green onions. Garnish with the remaining 1½ tablespoons sesame seeds, whole asparagus spears, and *shiso* leaves. Serve at room temperature.

Serves 10 to 12 as salad.

NOTE: To toast sesame seeds, place them in a small heavy frying pan over moderate heat. Stir until they begin to turn golden. Remove from heat and pour onto a plate to cool.

Curly Pasta with Vegetables in Green Mexican Salsa

15	fresh tomatillos, or 1 can (12 ounces) tomatillos, drained
2-3	fresh or canned hot chili peppers, seeded
1	clove garlic
1	cup chopped yellow onion
¼	cup chopped fresh coriander (cilantro)
¼	cup plus 2 tablespoons vegetable oil
1	pound long *fusilli* (curly long strands) or other fancifully shaped pasta
1	small red onion, chopped
2	medium-sized ripe tomatoes, chopped
1	large green or gold sweet pepper, chopped
1	cup cooked chopped prickly pear cactus leaves or *nopalitos* (see note)
½	cup finely minced fresh parsley or coriander (cilantro)
	Salt
½	cup freshly grated queso Chihuahua or Parmesan cheese
	Fresh coriander (cilantro) sprigs (garnish)
	Red onion, thinly sliced into rings and rings separated (garnish)

As an alternative to this festive buffet dish for any season, serve the pasta in halved avocados for the opening to a sit-down Mexican meal.

1. To make salsa, remove and disregard dry husk from fresh tomatillos, wash, and boil in water to cover until barely tender. Drain boiled or canned tomatillos and combine with chili peppers, garlic, yellow onion, and chopped coriander in a blender or food processor. Purée to chunky texture, about 5 seconds. Heat 2 tablespoons vegetable oil in a frying pan, add the tomatillo mixture, and cook, stirring constantly, for about 3 minutes. Set aside to cool.

2. Cook pasta in 4 quarts boiling water until very *al dente*. Drain and toss in a large bowl with remaining ¼ cup vegetable oil. Cool to room temperature, occasionally stirring the pasta to coat thoroughly.

3. Stir about half of the reserved salsa into the pasta. Add red onion, tomatoes, sweet pepper, cactus leaves, minced parsley or coriander, and salt to taste; mix thoroughly with your hands. Sprinkle with cheese; garnish with coriander sprigs and onion rings. Pass remaining salsa at the table.

Serves 10 to 12 as salad or first course.

NOTE: Prickly pear cactus leaves are available in markets that cater to Spanish populations. To prepare, carefully cut away the sharp spines with a paring knife. Dice the smooth cactus pad and simmer in salted water until tender. Drain and rinse in cold water to eliminate slippery juice. Prepared cactus leaves, called *nopalitos*, are also available in jars.

Pasta with Fresh Corn and Lima Beans in Apple Cider Vinaigrette

1   pound *spaghetti* or other pasta

¾   cup safflower oil

2   cups *each* cooked fresh corn kernels and cooked fresh or frozen lima beans

2   medium-sized tomatoes, peeled, seeded, and chopped

8   green onions, thinly sliced

6   strips thick-sliced bacon, crisply fried and crumbled

⅓   cup chopped fresh parsley

3   tablespoons cider vinegar

2   tablespoons freshly squeezed lemon juice

1   teaspoon granulated sugar

Salt

Freshly ground black pepper

Paprika

This salad was inspired by succotash, the combination of garden fresh corn and lima beans that has been a part of American cooking since colonial days.

1. Cook pasta in 4 quarts boiling water until very *al dente*. Drain and toss in a large bowl with ¼ cup safflower oil. Cool to room temperature, occasionally stirring the pasta to coat thoroughly.

2. Add corn, lima beans, tomatoes, onions, most of the bacon (reserve some for garnish), and parsley to pasta and mix well.

3. Combine the remaining ½ cup safflower oil with vinegar, lemon juice, sugar, and salt, pepper, and paprika to taste. Pour over pasta and blend thoroughly. Garnish with the reserved crumbled bacon.

Serves 10 to 12 as salad or side dish.

Corkscrew Pasta with Vegetables in Italian Vinaigrette

1	pound *fusilli* (corkscrew)
¾	cup olive oil
6	green onions, thinly sliced
1	red sweet pepper, finely chopped
2	carrots, peeled and coarsely shredded
3	yellow crookneck squash, coarsely chopped
1	pound fresh broccoli florets, blanched until just tender, then quickly cooled in ice water and drained
3	tablespoons minced fresh chives
1	cup firmly packed chopped fresh basil
1	cup freshly grated Parmesan cheese
1	tablespoon Dijon-style mustard
¼	cup balsamic vinegar
2–3	cloves garlic, minced
1	teaspoon granulated sugar
	Salt
	Freshly ground black pepper
	Crushed dried red pepper flakes
1	red sweet pepper, cut into thin julienne (garnish)
	Whole fresh basil leaves (garnish)
	Capers (garnish)

For a festive party dish in traditional Italian colors, use equal portions of spinach, egg, and tomato pastas. The tangy dressing goes perfectly with grilled or barbecued meats.

1. Cook pasta in 4 quarts boiling water until very *al dente*. Drain and toss in a large bowl with ¼ cup olive oil. Cool to room temperature, occasionally stirring the pasta to coat thoroughly.

2. Add green onions, chopped red pepper, carrots, squash, most of the broccoli florets (reserve a few for garnishing), chives, chopped basil, and ¾ cup cheese. Mix thoroughly with hands.

3. Whisk together mustard, vinegar, garlic, sugar, and salt, pepper, and red pepper flakes to taste. Continue to whisk while slowly dribbling in the remaining ½ cup olive oil. Pour over pasta and mix thoroughly.

4. Allow pasta to sit at room temperature for at least 2 hours or chill as long as overnight, then return to room temperature before serving. Garnish with pepper strips, reserved broccoli florets, basil leaves, the remaining ¼ cup Parmesan, and capers.

Serves 10 to 12 as salad or side dish.

Pasta with Gazpacho Dressing and Crunchy Vegetables

½   cup olive oil

½   cup red wine vinegar

2–3   cloves garlic, minced

½   teaspoon ground cumin

5   medium-sized ripe tomatoes, peeled, seeded, and chopped

2   medium-sized cucumbers, peeled, seeded, and chopped

      Salt

      Freshly ground black pepper

      Liquid hot pepper sauce

1   pound *tripolini* (tiny spoonlike bows) or other small pasta

2   gold or green sweet peppers, chopped

1   red onion, chopped

6–8   green onions, thinly sliced

1   cup black olives, preferably imported, pitted and sliced

1   cup chopped fresh parsley, preferably Italian

1   cup chopped fresh mint

Why not turn spicy soup vegetables into ingredients for a cold pasta? And as is often the case with the presentation of the soup of the same name, give diners a chance to choose their own toppings for this great party dish.

1. In a blender or food processor, combine olive oil, vinegar, garlic, cumin, about half the tomatoes and cucumbers, and salt, pepper, and pepper sauce to taste. Blend to a coarse purée and reserve.

2. Cook pasta in 4 quarts boiling water until very *al dente*. Drain and toss in a large bowl with about half the reserved salad dressing. Cool to room temperature, occasionally stirring the pasta to coat thoroughly.

3. Place pasta in a large shallow bowl. Put all remaining ingredients in small individual bowls and arrange around pasta bowl. Let everyone choose toppings at the table. Pass remaining salad dressing.

Serves 6 to 8 as main course; 10 to 12 as salad.

Spinach Pasta Primavera Verde

1	pound spinach pasta
¾	cup olive oil
2	cups shelled fresh green peas
½	pound fresh sugar snap peas or green beans, cut into thin julienne
1	pound fresh young asparagus, cut into 2-inch pieces
1	pound fresh broccoli, florets only
3	small zucchini, coarsely chopped
2	teaspoons Dijon-style mustard
3	tablespoons freshly squeezed lemon juice
2	tablespoons minced fresh tarragon, or 1 teaspoon dried tarragon leaves, crumbled
	Salt
	Freshly ground black pepper
2	cups slivered cooked turkey or baked ham
	Watercress sprigs (garnish)

Celebrate the arrival of spring with this all-green salad of spinach pasta and tiny garden vegetables.

1. Cook pasta in 4 quarts boiling water until very *al dente*. Drain and toss in a large bowl with ¼ cup olive oil. Cool to room temperature, occasionally stirring the pasta to coat thoroughly.

2. Separately blanch all the vegetables until just barely tender; immerse immediately in ice water. Drain well and add to pasta.

3. Combine mustard, lemon juice, tarragon, and salt and pepper to taste. Slowly whisk in the remaining ½ cup olive oil. Pour over pasta and mix well. Add turkey or ham if desired. Garnish with watercress.

Serves 10 to 12 as salad.

Chicken, Mein, and Vegetables
in Creamy Szechuan Dressing

1	pound thin *mein* (Chinese noodles)
¾	cup soy sauce
¼	cup peanut oil
2	cups mayonnaise
1	tablespoon Dijon-style mustard
¼	cup Oriental-style sesame oil
	Szechuan chili oil
2	whole chicken breasts
6	green onions, thinly sliced
2	carrots, peeled and coarsely chopped
1	red sweet pepper, coarsely chopped
1	can (8 ounces) sliced bamboo shoots, drained
1	jar (6 ounces) miniature corn on the cob, drained and thickly sliced
½	cup chopped fresh coriander (cilantro)
½	pound fresh snow peas, trimmed, cut into julienne, and blanched until crisp-tender, then cooled in ice water and drained
	Fresh coriander (cilantro) sprigs (garnish)
	Lightly toasted sesame seeds (see note; garnish)

I first concocted this dish for Kristi and Bob Spence at Lake Tahoe, and it has since become my favorite summer lunch or picnic fare. The flavor of the dish improves from an overnight chilling, but wait until the last minute to add the crunchy snow peas. Please be very generous with the chili oil; cold noodles can take a lot of heat.

1. Skin, bone, and halve chicken breasts. Poach and cool according to directions on page 93. Cut into bite-sized pieces and reserve.

2. Cook noodles in 4 quarts boiling water until very *al dente*. Drain and toss in a large bowl with ½ cup soy sauce, then peanut oil. Cool to room temperature, occasionally stirring the noodles to coat thoroughly.

3. Combine mayonnaise with mustard, sesame oil, the remaining ¼ cup soy sauce, and chili oil to taste. Refrigerate until ready to use.

4. Add reserved chicken, green onions, carrots, sweet pepper, bamboo shoots, miniature corn, and chopped coriander to noodles. Mix gently, but thoroughly with hands. Add the reserved mayonnaise mixture and blend well. Cover and refrigerate until ready to serve, preferably overnight.

5. About 30 minutes before serving time, remove noodle mixture from refrigerator and toss in julienned snow peas, adding a little extra soy sauce and peanut oil or mayonnaise if the noodles seem dry. Garnish with coriander sprigs and sesame seeds. Pass additional soy sauce and chili oil at the table.

Serves 6 as main course; 10 to 12 as salad.

NOTE: To toast sesame seeds, place them in a small heavy frying pan over moderate heat. Stir until seeds are golden. Remove from heat and pour onto a plate to cool.

Pasta Shells with Crab Meat and West Coast Louis Dressing

1	pound small pasta shells
3	cups homemade mayonnaise
¼	cup freshly squeezed lemon juice
2	tablespoons grated onion
½	cup bottled chili sauce
1	tablespoon Worcestershire sauce
2	tablespoons prepared horseradish
	Salt
	Freshly ground black pepper
	Cayenne pepper
1	head firm lettuce, finely shredded
1½	pounds cooked crab meat, flaked
2	cups *each* peeled and sliced carrots and celery, blanched till just tender, then quickly cooled in ice water and drained
	Lemon wedges or slices (garnish)
	Watercress sprigs (garnish)

This new variation of the longtime Pacific coast favorite is best when made with fresh crab, although frozen Alaska king crab meat is acceptable. Shrimps or prawns are also tasty additions to or substitutes for crab.

1. Cook pasta in 4 quarts boiling water until very *al dente*. Drain and rinse well in cold water, then drain again. Place in a large bowl and cool to room temperature, stirring occasionally to keep pasta from sticking together.

2. Combine mayonnaise, lemon juice, onion, chili sauce, Worcestershire sauce, horseradish, and salt, black pepper, and cayenne pepper to taste. Add about 1 cup of the dressing to the cooled pasta and toss gently. Chill remaining dressing and the pasta until just before serving time, up to 3 hours. Remove pasta from refrigerator about 20 minutes before serving time.

3. Arrange shredded lettuce on chilled plates. Add pasta and top with crab, carrots, and celery. Garnish with lemon and watercress. Pass chilled dressing at the table.

Serves 6 as main course; 8 to 10 as salad.

Beef Fillet with Macaroni in Shallot-Mustard Dressing

12	ounces elbow or spiral-shaped macaroni
2	tablespoons hazelnut or walnut oil
2	cups julienned cooked beef fillet (1-inch-wide strips)
⅓	cup finely minced fresh parsley
2	tablespoons finely chopped fresh chives
2	tablespoons *each* Dijon-style mustard and red wine vinegar
½	teaspoon granulated sugar
1	large shallot, finely minced
	Salt
	Freshly ground black pepper
¼	cup olive oil
	Pickled onions (garnish)
	Yellow mustard seeds or black peppercorns (garnish)

Radicchio or lettuce cups would be appropriate holders for this hearty salad.

1. Cook pasta in 3 quarts boiling water until very *al dente*. Drain and toss in a large bowl with hazelnut or walnut oil. Cool to room temperature, occasionally stirring the pasta to coat thoroughly.

2. Add beef, parsley, and chives to pasta and mix thoroughly.

3. Whisk together mustard, vinegar, sugar, shallot, and salt and pepper to taste. Slowly whisk in olive oil. Pour over pasta and mix thoroughly. Garnish with pickled onions and mustard seeds or peppercorns.

Serves 4 as main course; 6 to 8 as salad.

Vermicelli with Shrimp in Curried Yogurt

1	pound *vermicelli* (very fine rods) or other thin pasta
¼	cup vegetable oil
1–2	small fresh hot chili peppers, finely minced
1	red or green sweet pepper, chopped
6	green onions, thinly sliced
2	cups cooked tiny shrimps, shelled and deveined
1½	cups plain yogurt
¼	cup canned cream of coconut
2	tablespoons freshly squeezed lemon or lime juice
2–3	tablespoons curry powder (hot or mild according to taste)
2	cloves garlic, finely minced or pressed
2	teaspoons minced fresh ginger
	Salt
	Freshly ground black pepper
	Fresh mango, peeled and sliced (garnish)
	Unsweetened grated coconut (garnish)
	Unsalted dry-roasted peanuts (garnish)
	Fresh mint leaves (garnish)

Perhaps suprisingly, vermicelli is a traditional part of Indian cuisine, as are the other ingredients of this sweet-spicy dish, but the idea is purely California.

1. Cook pasta in 4 quarts boiling water until very *al dente*. Drain and rinse well in cold water, then drain again. Place in a large bowl and cool to room temperature, stirring occasionally to keep pasta from sticking together.

2. Add chili pepper, sweet pepper, onions, and shrimps to pasta and mix well.

3. Combine yogurt, cream of coconut, lemon juice, curry powder, garlic, ginger, and salt and pepper to taste; mix with pasta. Garnish pasta with mango, grated coconut, peanuts, and mint leaves.

Serves 6 to 8 as main course; 10 to 12 as salad.

Pasta with Poached Meats and Vegetables in Garlic Aïoli

12	cloves garlic, finely minced or pressed
3	egg yolks
2	tablespoons freshly squeezed lemon juice
¼	cup hazelnut oil (optional)
1½	cups olive oil, or 1¾ cups if hazelnut oil is not used
	Salt
	Freshly ground white pepper
1	pound *creste di gallo* (cockscomb) or other fancifully shaped pasta
2	large leeks, thinly sliced
½	pound fresh green beans, cut into 2-inch pieces
2	carrots, peeled and cut into julienne (2-inch matchsticks)
½	head cauliflower, broken or cut into bite-sized florets
3	tablespoons minced fresh parsley, preferably Italian
1	cup cooked small artichoke hearts, quartered
1	whole chicken breast, skinned, boned, halved, poached, and sliced into ½ inch-wide strips
1	pound prawns, cooked, shelled, and deveined
4	hard-cooked eggs, peeled and sliced

This dish is based on aïoli, a classic Mediterranean garlic sauce normally used for dipping poached meats and vegetables. The sauce can be made a day ahead, refrigerated, and returned to room temperature before mixing into pasta.

1. In a blender or food processor, combine garlic, raw egg yolks, and lemon juice and blend well. With motor running at high speed, slowly drizzle in hazelnut and olive oils and blend until thick. Add salt and white pepper to taste. Refrigerate until needed.

2. Cook pasta in 4 quarts boiling water until very *al dente*. Drain and rinse well in cold water, then drain again. Place in a large bowl and cool to room temperature, stirring occasionally to keep pasta from sticking together.

3. Separately blanch leeks, green beans, carrots, and cauliflower florets until crisp-tender, then cool immediately in ice water. Drain well.

4. Add parsley, blanched leeks, and about half of the aïoli sauce to the pasta and mix well.

5. Place the pasta on individual plates or a large serving tray and surround with groupings of the beans, carrots, cauliflower, artichoke hearts, chicken strips, prawns, and hard-cooked eggs. Offer remaining aïoli at the table.

Serves 6 to 8 as main course; 10 to 12 as salad.

Duck Breast and Pasta
in Hazelnut-Raspberry Dressing

2   teaspoons Dijon-style or
green peppercorn mustard

2   tablespoons raspberry
vinegar
Salt
Freshly ground
black pepper

1   tablespoon olive oil

2   tablespoons hazelnut oil

8   ounces *spaghettini* (very
thin rods) or other thin pasta

1   whole duck breast, boned,
trimmed of excess fat, and
cut in half (roast the duck
legs for another meal)

2   tablespoons minced fresh
parsley, preferably Italian

3   green onions,
or 1 medium-sized leek,
cut into julienne
(2-inch matchsticks)
Lightly toasted hazelnuts
(see note; garnish)
Fresh raspberries (garnish)
Green peppercorns
(garnish)

Succulent duck breast tops pasta tossed in raspberry-hazelnut vinaigrette. Prepare shortly before serving at room temperature.

1. Combine mustard, vinegar, and salt and pepper to taste and blend well. Slowly whisk in olive and hazelnut oils. Set aside.

2. Cook pasta in 4 quarts boiling water until very *al dente*. Drain and toss in a large bowl with reserved vinaigrette dressing. Cool to room temperature, occasionally stirring the pasta to coat thoroughly.

3. In a medium-sized frying pan over moderately high heat, sauté duck breast, skin side down, until skin is browned, 7 to 8 minutes. Pour off fat. Turn and sauté until bottom of breast is lightly browned, 2 to 3 minutes. Remove and cool. Reserve skin and cut meat into thin slices. Cover and set aside.

4. Slice duck skin into long thin strips. Return skin to pan and cook until crisp and golden brown, about 10 minutes. Remove with a slotted spoon and drain on paper toweling.

5. Add parsley to pasta and mix well. Place pasta on individual plates, sprinkle with green onion or leek, and top with sliced duck. Garnish with toasted hazelnuts, raspberrries, and peppercorns. Serve immediately at room temperature; do not refrigerate.

Serves 2 to 3 as main course; 4 to 6 as salad.

NOTE: To toast hazelnuts, place them in a small heavy frying pan in a 350° F oven. Stir frequently until they are lightly browned. Remove from oven and pour onto a plate to cool. Rub between fingers to remove husk.

Pasta with Muffalata Olive Salad and Italian Meats

1½	cups chopped pimiento-stuffed green olives
1	cup chopped pitted Greek olives
¼	cup juice from olives
½	cup chopped canned pimiento
1	cup pickled *giardiniera* (mixed Italian vegetables) drained and chopped
2	cloves garlic, minced
3	anchovy fillets, minced
2	tablespoons capers
¾	cup minced fresh parsley
1	tablespoon minced fresh oregano, or 1 teaspoon dried oregano leaves
	Crushed dried red pepper flakes
⅔	cup olive oil
1	pound *gnocchi*-shaped (dumpling-shaped) pasta
¼	pound thinly sliced mortadella, cut into julienne
⅛	pound thinly sliced prosciutto, cut into julienne
¼	pound provolone or jack cheese, cut into small cubes
¼	pound Italian salami, thinly sliced
	Whole Greek olives (garnish)

New Orleans's famous muffuletta sandwich features a filling of olive salad and Italian meats that seems a natural for dressing cold pasta. When offered at the beginning of an Italian meal, it takes the place of both antipasto and pasta.

1. Combine chopped olives, olive juice, pimiento, *giardiniera*, garlic, anchovies, capers, minced parsley, oregano, crushed red pepper to taste, and olive oil. Let stand overnight.

2. Cook pasta in 4 quarts boiling water until very *al dente*. Drain and toss in a large bowl with olive salad mixture. Cool to room temperature, occasionally stirring the pasta to coat thoroughly.

3. Add mortadella, prosciutto, and cheese to pasta. Serve with salami on side and garnish with a few whole olives.

Serves 6 to 8 as main course; 12 as antipasto or salad.

Bow Ties with Chicken and White Vegetables in Garlic Mayonnaise

2	cups homemade mayonnaise
3	cloves or more garlic, minced
2	jars (6 ounces *each*) marinated artichoke hearts, drained (reserve oil) and sliced
1	pound *farfalle* (medium-sized bows)
1	can (7 to 8 ounces) hearts of palm, drained and sliced
2	whole chicken breasts, skinned, boned, halved, poached, and cut into bite-sized pieces
4	heads Belgian endive, leaves separated
	Pink pepperberries (dried fruit of *Schinus molle* tree; garnish)

Based on the popular chicken salad from Twin Peaks Grocery in San Francisco, all-white ingredients give this delicious combination an elegant appearance appropriate for your grandest dinner party. It's equally wonderful as picnic fare.

1. Combine mayonnaise with garlic and oil drained from marinated artichokes. Chill.

2. Cook pasta in 4 quarts boiling water until very *al dente*. Drain and rinse well in cold water, then drain again. Place in a large bowl and cool to room temperature, stirring occasionally to keep pasta from sticking together.

3. To prevent tearing pasta shape, use hands to gently blend about one-third of the garlic-flavored mayonnaise with the pasta. Chill as long as overnight. Remove from refrigerator about 30 minutes before serving.

4. Combine artichoke hearts, hearts of palm, chicken, and remaining garlic-flavored mayonnaise. Chill as long as overnight. Remove from refrigerator about 30 minutes before serving.

5. Line individual plates with endive leaves. Spoon pasta bows atop lower half of the leaves and arrange artichoke heart mixture alongside. Garnish with pink pepperberries.

Serves 6 to 8 as main course; 10 to 12 as salad.

Pasta with Fresh Fruits and Yogurt

2 cups mixed berries (blackberries, blueberries, raspberries, strawberries)

1½ cups mixed melon balls (cantaloupe, crenshaw, honeydew)

2 cups sliced seasonal fruits (figs, grapes, kiwis, mangoes, nectarines, peaches)
Honey or granulated sugar

1 cup freshly squeezed orange juice

2 tablespoons freshly squeezed lemon juice

½ cup bourbon or orange-flavored liqueur

12 ounces *tubetti* (small tubes) or other small macaroni

2 cups plain yogurt

¾ cup coarsely chopped pecans or other nuts
Shaved semisweet or bittersweet chocolate (optional)
Fresh mint leaves (garnish)

Sounds strange? Actually, the combination proves a delicious low-calorie dessert or salad lunch (minus the chocolate).

1. Combine all the fruits in a large bowl. Drizzle with honey or sprinkle with sugar to taste. Pour orange and lemon juices and bourbon or liqueur over fruits, cover, and refrigerate for several hours.

2. Cook the pasta in 3 quarts boiling water until very *al dente*. Drain and rinse well in cold water, then drain again. Place in a large bowl and cool to room temperature, stirring occasionally to keep pasta from sticking together.

3. Stir about ¼ cup honey or sugar into yogurt and toss well with pasta. Refrigerate if not served immediately, removing from refrigerator about 25 minutes before serving. To serve, surround pasta with fruits and sprinkle with nuts. If this is to be dessert, top with chocolate. In either case, garnish with mint.

Serves 6 to 8 as salad or dessert.

Vermicelli with Nuts and Sweet Spices

3	tablespoons whipping cream
½	teaspoon saffron threads
½	cup (1 stick) butter
6	whole cloves
5	whole cardamom pods
2	teaspoons ground ginger
1	pound *vermicelli* (very fine rods) or other thin pasta, broken into 2-inch lengths
1	cup milk
¾	cup granulated sugar
¼	cup sliced blanched almonds
⅓	cup coarsely chopped pistachios
	Fresh fruit

We are so accustomed to beginning meals with pasta that this super-sweet adaptation of a traditional Muslim feast-day dish can be an unexpected reversal.

1. Bring cream almost to a boil and add saffron. Remove from heat and let stand at least 20 minutes.

2. Heat butter in a large frying pan over medium heat. Add cloves, cardamom, and ginger and cook, stirring occasionally, until the pods open. Add the pasta, reduce heat to low, and cook, stirring frequently, until it turns deep golden brown, about 15 minutes.

3. Add milk, 1 cup water, and sugar. Stirring occasionally, cook until the liquid has been absorbed and the pasta is soft but still a little chewy, about 25 minutes.

4. Turn pasta onto a serving dish. Sprinkle with reserved saffron cream and garnish with nuts. Cool to room temperature before serving. Accompany with fresh fruit.

Serves 8 to 10 as dessert.

Noodle Pudding with Vanilla Bean Sauce

8	ounces medium-width egg noodles
3	eggs, well beaten
1	cup cottage cheese
¾	cup firmly packed brown sugar
1	cup chunky applesauce, preferably homemade
¾	cup golden raisins
1	cup coarsely chopped walnuts or pecans
4	teaspoons ground cinnamon
1	teaspoon *each* ground cloves and freshly grated nutmeg
½	cup melted butter
1	teaspoon salt
1	tablespoon vanilla extract or bourbon
1	vanilla bean, or 2 teaspoons vanilla extract
2	cups whipping cream
4	egg yolks
¼	cup granulated sugar
1	tablespoon bourbon (optional)
	Green apple, diced and tossed in freshly squeezed lemon juice, or homemade chunky applesauce (garnish)
	Freshly grated nutmeg (garnish)

If you enjoy custards as much as I do, double the creamy sauce. Without the sauce, this not-overly-sweet dessert makes a good side dish with cold roasts for outdoor dining.

1. Cook pasta in 2 quarts boiling water until very *al dente*. Drain and rinse thoroughly in cold water, then drain again. Place in a large bowl and cool to room temperature, stirring occasionally to keep pasta from sticking together.

2. Combine eggs, cottage cheese, brown sugar, applesauce, raisins, nuts, cinnamon, ground cloves, nutmeg, butter, salt, and 1 tablespoon vanilla extract or bourbon. Mix thoroughly with pasta. Pour into a well-greased 1-quart pudding mold or springform pan. Cover top of pudding very loosely with foil. Bake at 350° F until set, about 1 hour.

3. Cool pudding slightly and invert onto plate, or remove from springform pan and slide upright onto a plate. Cool to room temperature; chill in refrigerator.

4. Meanwhile, place the vanilla bean in the cream in a small saucepan over medium heat and bring almost to a boil. Remove from the heat. Beat egg yolks in the top pan of a double boiler placed over barely simmering water. Slowly beat in granulated sugar, continuing to beat until mixture is pale yellow and thick. Gradually whisk in heated cream along with vanilla bean and cook, stirring constantly, until thickened, about 10 minutes. Remove from the heat and take out the vanilla bean (save for another use); if using vanilla extract instead of the bean stir it in at this point. Add 1 tablespoon bourbon if desired. Cool to room temperature, stirring occasionally. Cover surface with piece of plastic wrap to prevent crust from forming and refrigerate until well chilled.

5. To serve, slice the noodle pudding and place on a pool of the sauce, or pass the sauce to pour over the pudding at the table. Garnish with apple slices or a bit of applesauce and a sprinkling of nutmeg.

Serves 8 to 10 as dessert.

MAYONNAISE

1   whole egg
      (at room temperature)
2   egg yolks
      (at room temperature)
1   tablespoon Dijon-style
      mustard
3   tablespoons freshly
      squeezed lemon juice
2   cups safflower or other
      vegetable oil
      Salt

Homemade mayonnaise is generally preferred to store-bought because of its superior freshness, but as I'm often in a hurry when making cold pastas, I usually reach for a jar of high-quality commercial "real" mayonnaise. The flavor of these jarred alternatives is improved by adding a bit of freshly squeezed lemon juice. If you want to make your own mayonnaise, this recipe yields enough to prepare any dish in this book.

1. In a blender or food processor fitted with a steel blade, combine egg, egg yolks, mustard, and lemon juice. Blend for about 30 seconds.

2. With motor running, add oil in a slow, steady stream. When mayonnaise thickens, turn motor off. With a rubber or plastic spatula, scrape oil from sides of container and blend into mayonnaise. Taste and add salt and more lemon juice, if desired. Transfer mayonnaise to a covered container and store in the refrigerator for up to 5 days. Always allow mayonnaise to reach room temperature before adding it to pasta.

Makes about 3 cups.

VARIATION: For Italian *maionese*, delete mustard and substitute olive oil for safflower or vegetable oil.

SZECHUAN CHILI OIL

If you can't find this liquid fire on the shelves of nearby Oriental markets, make your own version. Though extremely hot, use generously in the recipes in this book. Cold pasta absorbs a lot of heat.

1. Place at least 2 or 3 tablespoons Szechuan peppercorns or crushed dried hot red chili peppers in a pint-sized bottle or jar and fill with peanut or vegetable oil. Let stand for at least 2 weeks before using.

Makes 1 pint.

POACHED CHICKEN BREASTS

Succulent poached chicken is essential to the success of several recipes in this book. The easy poaching method that follows works well.

1. Place skinned, boned, and halved chicken breasts in a frying pan or saucepan in which they fit comfortably. Add just enough cold water or white wine to cover.

2. Bring to a boil and immediately reduce heat so water barely ripples. Simmer breasts until they are done, about 12 to 15 minutes. The meat should be moist and opaque white throughout; cook only to just beyond the pink stage.

3. Remove breasts with a slotted spoon and drain well. Cool to room temperature before using as directed in recipes.

Index